Kiko,
Read this on your travels. *sends that last email* lol.
Much love,

THE BLACK BUTTERFLY ANTHOLOGY

The

Black Butterfly

Anthology

Deonne Pennant

Illustrations by Daria Modlinska
Book cover by Rita Pennant

ISBN: 9781980236047

THE BLACK BUTTERFLY ANTHOLOGY

THE BLACK BUTTERFLY ANTHOLOGY

I wrote stories to escape,
I write poetry now I'm free.

– *Deonne*

Acknowledgement

In recognition of the Dyslexia Association's assistance in helping me to overcome my struggles.
Without them, I would not have climbed the mountain and the outlook would have been so different. I hope this book can be an encouragement to others.

Contents

Dyscalculia

Maths, ugh actually don't want to go there.

Probably the only subject that could give me a scare.

I hated it.

I detested it.

Maybe those feelings don't quite describe, the

feelings of frustration when I couldn't get it right.

People would wonder how I was good with words

but when it came to maths it was like another

world.

After every maths lesson, I only wanted to cry

because I couldn't understand, and I didn't know

why.

A bit like algebra, what's x and what's y?

Funny how when you're a child, you're clever to know
what's wrong.

And for me, it really didn't take long.

A few years later when the diagnostics was done,

I felt relief; not to be labelled

but to have found some

justice and realisation to why

I did things a different way.

I will always be extremely thankful

to my mom and for that day;

and to those who supported me in every single way.

So, to those out there with learning difficulties;

whether the issues are known or unknown,

you are neither dumb nor stupid and you don't have to go

through it alone.

Dreams are worth dreaming

Dreams are worth dreaming and worth believing
so don't let anything stop you from achieving.
Believe you can with all your heart and keep
pushing forward even in the difficult part.
For even the greatest of greats were just like you
once.

Blossom

Blossom into the person who wiped your tears
away when you thought you'd lost everything.
Blossom into the person who gave you their time
to spare so you could voice your problems.
Blossom into the person who held your hand
when you were afraid to walk the path alone.
Blossom into the person who spread joy to your
heart when
it was burdened.
Blossom into the person who believed in you
when you had no faith in yourself.
Blossom into the person who made you see the
rainbow on your darkest days on earth.
Blossom into the person who spoke good of you
even when you were acting the worst.
Blossom into the person who put themselves
second and you first.
*Because a flower is most beautiful once bloomed
and it's scent and feel does not last forever.*

Fragile hearts

Sometimes it's the people
who look like they have the pieces stuck together
who have had the glass of their hearts
shattered the most.

Stand up

Stand up for what you believe in.
Stand up for what is right.
We're all entitled to our opinions
but the kind that involves words
and not fights.

If not for me

If not for me
then do it for you;
be the happiest.

We'll always stick together

Some friends are temporary, but family is
forever.
Sometimes life is bad and other times it's
better.
Sometimes life can switch up like the seasons;
like the weather.
But one thing that's certain,
is we'll always stick together.

The beautiful things

The moon doesn't complain about it being too dark
to shine.
Or that the stars might steal it's spotlight.

The sun doesn't complain about how the people on
the earth are not deserving of its pleasurable heat.
Or how it sometimes must finish its job midday
and hide behind the clouds, so the rain can come
out.

The flower doesn't complain about how the little
girls pluck and tear away its petals to
decorate their heads and wrists.

And the earth doesn't complain when the pollution
destroys the air it needs.

Sometimes it's the beautiful things that we take
longer to notice.
Sometimes it's the beautiful things that need the
most care
because sometimes,
just sometimes,
it's the most beautiful things that have been
through the very worst.

Dahlia

I am like none of the others
that blossom in the garden.
My petals, they are delicate,
they are unique, they are beautiful.
My petals are symmetrical, mesmerising
and full of colour.
Pink, orange, white,
blue, yellow or red.
A work of art is what they call me.
A beauty is what they say.
No matter the day, I stay stunning,
waving in the air of the summer
light.

A once a week father

Your lips curl back wide,
like they're trying to paint the happiness across
your entire face.
And your eyes, they squint up,
like shrivelled shiny raisins;
the ones I like to pick
out of hot cross buns during the Easter holidays.
And your laugh; it makes me laugh –
so full, so content
and so cheery.
I must have a secret power because
you're never like this with mom.
I wish you could be as happy as this more often.
I wish that I could see you more often.
I'm happy with you, father.
It's a shame I only see you once a week.

Finding your own personality

That's the problem with people nowadays.
We're all trying to be the same in a world that craves
originality.
When really, we need to find ourselves and reveal our
personality.

Pink Himalayan salt

Pink Himalayan salt.
I'd search for it.
I've heard it's deep within the mountains.
I'll search for it.
I've heard it's the purest form of salt in the
world, full of colour,
full of minerals.
I'll find it.
Sprinkle it into my life
So I can become immune
to all the bad things that
happen.

This generation of attention

What is wrong with our generation?
We're such attention seekers; we must think that's our
way of knowing that we're loved.
"Put me on your story if I mean anything to you." or
"He didn't text back within a minute, what am I
supposed to do?!"
What is wrong with our generation?
What happened to us learning how to work and invest
time into a person called 'You'?
We hear the gossip and the mistruths
which start the arguments and the lies.
We want to know whose still friends with who
and which couple will cut ties?
The world is far too big to be the centre of it all
or to be concerned with such matters trivial.
Just focus on the little things,
the important things and not what the minority of
people think about you or say about you.
Life's too short to be a member of this generation
of attention.
There are so many more things in life that need your
time and comprehension.

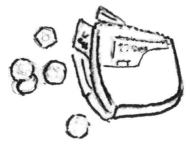

Are you rich?

I say that I am rich.

I have little money but plenty of love.

Player

You weren't there for me like I was there for you.
Your words didn't match the actions that you said you
were going to do.
You kept me waiting for something like it was a game.
You played me and won, and you put me to shame.
But next time I won't be so naïve.
I will find the strength to leave.

Midwinter

Cold feet.

Cold hands.

Cracked lips.

Icy breeze.

Frozen.

Wet.

The doubts

All I ever do is doubt myself and where
has that gotten me?
It's taken me on a journey to places
I don't even want to be.
But this time,
I won't let Them control me.
I'm not going to doubt myself anymore.

I'm a social vegetarian

I'm a social vegetarian.
I stay away from all the beef.
I stay away from the trouble makers;
the secret tea leafs.
Because
sometimes in life it's hard to trust others,
especially when the liars are your own brothers.

Being real

Be you.
Be true.
And do what you gotta do.

Our kind of love

Tell me about your nights and how many stars you
count.
And how many dreams you dream.
Does your leg fall gracefully out of the covers to
feel the air that flows through your window at
night?

And tell me about your mornings.
And how many coffees you drink to stop the yawnings.
Let's start conversations over the little things.
                    That's our kind of love.

Why?

People nowadays want a first-class
seat in your business.
They want to see your every move
and deny themselves their
happiness.
And for what?
And for who?
Don't they have their own life too?

Don't hide, butterfly

Some people are like butterflies; they shine, dazzle,
and skip through life
oblivious to their beauty within and on the outside.
And when you tell them just how full of colour they
are; they try to find a place to vanish, to cover, to hide.

Please don't judge me

Please don't judge me. Accept me as I am.
I am a book with words that fill the entire page.
Read me and understand.
I am a sky that holds more stars than you will ever
see.
Look up and make a wish.
I am greater than you thought before you judged me.
Give me a chance.

A better future

Don't let the past grow hands and get a hold on you.
Don't let the hurt or the pain or the hate, stop you
from being able to create a better future for you.

Why we never worked out

All I wanted was a text back.
All I wanted was a call.
All I wanted was a tight hug.
All I wanted was to give you my all.
But I guess I forgot, we show our love
in different ways.
And maybe,
just maybe
that's why we never worked out.

Keep smiling

Smile. Even when your heart is frowning.

Laugh. Even if you're burdened with sadness.

Love. Even if your heart is broken.

Cry. Even if you want to hide away.

But live,

even if you think things won't get better,
because happy minds make happy lives.

Realize their worth

Why is it that good people always get hurt?
They're treated like dirt and left broken.
It's like no one wants to hear their side of the story
spoken. People say that they love too easily; too hard
and they fall too deep.
When really, they just want to spread love and
happiness; what you sow you shall reap.
People say they're too loyal but is there such a
thing? Because everyone wants a hand to hold when
words can't mend their wounds because they only
sting.
People say they trust too much and, in the end,
they're the ones left weeping and in pain but was it
their fault for trying to be the sunshine to your day,
when in your mind it was just earthquakes and rain.
Why is it that good people always get hurt?
It's because they give their love freely and get
treated like dirt but hold on to the hope that one day
you'll realize their worth.

Life's like a lamp

Life is like a light; shining bright each day

within you;

reminding you that the shadows of your past

will never be as bright as your

Future.

I promise you rainbows

You say that people always end up walking away.
But not me;
I'm here to stay.
I promise.
When you're sad, there's not a tear that I won't miss.
I'll catch them before they fall so,
on your rainy days you'll see rainbows.
I promise.

Bitter

Make me a fresh cup of tea.
Steamy, milky, and sweet,
like your personality.
The one I miss,
before you started drinking coffee.
Steamy, dark, and dull.

The past

No one should make you feel bad.
You're worth more than that.
I know it's hard to talk about, but it will get
easier; you have to go through the hard times to
get to the good. Even if you're afraid of being
misunderstood.

Like a wildfire

Appreciate all the kindness around you and all the love.
Then pass it on like wildfire.

Head up high

Onwards and upwards they say but your mind is still stuck in the past. You talk about how you've moved on; slammed the door of your history in it's face, but you've only run away from it all. Emotionally, you're still in a similar place, just a page forward. It's like you've read a book but just can't stop re-reading the same page.

Don't kid yourself into thinking that you're over it when the memories still return bringing hurt and pain to your mind and soul, or when tears prick the inside of your eyes. This is a result of your past which you'll sooner know how to escape from, mentally.

You're in control now. Take your time. Step by step. It takes time to grow into a new you. Block out the people that say you should be 'over it' by now and forgive them because they just don't understand. But let those in who care for you and who show they can make time for you. They will understand and maybe they won't know what to do but they will have your back. They will offer a hand to help and an ear to listen and that's enough - More than enough. You have to work on yourself, build yourself back up till you restore your peace of mind. You may not be exactly the person that you were before but surely this new person you are on the path to becoming is worth the effort to see. You have to believe that because you have not made it this far just to give up and return to the damaged you; the one who walked around with internal plasters and external smiles. Look forwards and not backwards. Until you can be truthfully honest with yourself about not letting what happened pave your way in life, that's when you can say onwards and upwards with your mind solely rooted in the Present and the Future. And what great things They have to offer. It's like reading a book and not dismissing any part of it because you know the resolution would not be the way it was without the beginning and the middle but accepting it and reading the sequel none the less. Your past is irreversible and there's nothing you can do about that, but your future – you're already on the way towards it and I don't think you've ever looked better than you do now; keep your head up high.

Vibes

Let's vibe till the sunrise.

And the sun sets.

How would you describe us?

What we have, it's something special
like when a friendly face asks, "Do you want tea?
I'll put the kettle on."
Like when a mother cradles her child and sings him
a lullaby;
Like when a friend wipes her friends tears and tells
her not to cry;
Like when a soldier returns from war and reunites
with his family;
Like when the young sweetheart couple get married
and live happily;
Like when your father tucks you into bed at night;
Like when you've walked in the dark for some
time, but God finally shows you the light.
That is how I would describe us.

Life's challenges

Sometimes life throws you challenges that you would
least expect.
But maybe it's just a trial to help make you the best.

What if I was made of glass?

What if I was made of glass?
Or fine china, to be exact.
Would you 'handle me with care' then?
Or watch me try and put myself back together?

I want to fall in love with an artist

I want to fall in love with an artist.
Someone who sees the galaxies in my eyes and
envisions fairy dust for my aura. Someone who will tell
me that when my lips curl into a smile, my face will
twinkle and shine brighter than the brightest star in the
sky.

Someone who will see my complexion as the deepest,
sweetest mahogany they have ever seen. And see my
black curls as precious jewels on a tiara. Someone who
will treat my imperfections and flaws like words on
paper, waiting to be understood.

I want to fall in love with an artist.
Simply because they will be the one person who will
love me for me, on days I don't even love myself. For
an artist is still an artist whether their canvas is
splattered with paint or not.

Writing after midnight

I wrote this at 12:00

I wrote that at 12:01

Teenage

Friends, they're more like family. We have banter
and I can talk to them whenever I need to. Music is
my best friend though. My favourite room at home is
the kitchen – the fridge, specifically,
Then my bedroom; my bed, specifically.
It's not a tantrum, it's called being annoyed so yes,
I'm going to slam that door. And don't call me
antisocial because I'm on my phone socialising on my
socials. Hungry 24/7. Yes, I skipped breakfast…not
the point.
I live with my parents; they are just the pair that pay
the rent. Sometimes I feel like that, other days I love
them both more. Deep down, every day I do, I just
don't always show it. Chores to do? Talk about slave
labour; can't get enough of it…not. Don't roll your
eyes!
Have you done your homework? Why aren't you
sleeping, you've got school tomorrow? I'll take a nap
tomorrow.
They're just a friend, nothing more, it's not like
we're dating. Don't start hating. I can't wait till lunch.
How long
do we have till school ends? All this stressing isn't
good for my health. How is there another test
tomorrow? You haven't done it either? I'll say I'm ill.
Mom, Dad, I love you. (also, what's the password
for the WIFI?)

Changes

We claim to be making all these changes;
changes to the world that we live in,
changes to the things that we believe in.
But are we really getting to where we need to be?
the place that we all envisioned,
the place that we dreamed to see.
Nowadays, we're trying to erase the past
instead of learning from the things
we did or where we were last.
We claim that we want racism to stop
and that now it is all over
but there are still strong black men being pulled
over by the police for their melanin
and getting shot for what? For anything!
We claim to want equality but even the
working citizens are in poverty.
We claim to have democracy
yet people are coming forward now after years of
secrecy.
Changes?
Tell me what changes we are making?

Feather

You felt like a feather; floaty and light
and unable to control where
your next destination would be.
Or where you would fall.
But through it all,
you kept holding on.
You knew that things were going to get better.

A world of our own

We are allowed to escape into a world of our
own.
A world not governed by the ticking of time.
A world simply invented by ourselves.
For ourselves.
We are never lonely, no matter how much our
minds try to trick us into thinking that we are.
We are merely appreciating ourselves,
indulging in our surroundings,
counting our blessings.
Realising that being alone is
an underestimated strength,
an overlooked gift,
a beautiful concept,
not to be confused with not having friends.

And time keeps ticking by

I met a boy once.
He was afraid.
I don't know what of, to be honest. I'm not sure.
He talked of all the wonders that manifested in his
mind like shooting stars in the galaxy, rainbows with
pots of gold at the end, splattered canvases with blues
and ivy and his eyes would flash bright at the
thoughts.
These wonders were filled with magnificent visions
of who he wanted to become and what he wanted to
do with his life.
And he talked about fitting in; into groups that all
looked and acted and spoke the same.
He claimed he was a chameleon, but he was talking
about his mind.
His mind was so clogged with 'their opinions' and
'their thoughts' that he couldn't think for himself.
His own thoughts were something he had to chase to
find. I think he was afraid that Time might catch up
with him and swallow his thoughts first and then
return to swallow him whole.
But I'm not sure.
All I know is that
he was so afraid
and trapped
and wrapped up
in the imagination of his own mind that
he never got the chance to ever make his dreams a
reality.

And I tried my best,
my very best to help him.
I told him, Time is cruel. It doesn't wait for
anyone and it doesn't lend you time to catch up
with the past.
It forces you to keep moving forward
and I think that is what he didn't understand.
Because now, I spend time thinking about who he
could have been and how the beautiful ideas of his
mind would look if only he had shown them when he
could.
And I always remember that I knew a boy once and
he was afraid.
I don't know what of, to be honest.
And I don't think he knew either.
And Time keeps ticking by.

Sunlight

You remind me of sunlight;
warm, bright
satisfying my mind
.

You'll get there

There's so much pressure to do better;
to be the best you can be;
to reach for the stars that you see.

You'll get there.

Is this real?

This affection. This connection.
Is it real?
Or am I just a part of your collection?
Like a tragic story on your bookshelf
that everyone knows the ending to.
Except me.

We were young

We were young.
Yet our unspoken
words of affection
and passion lay hidden
in the creases of our eyes,
our cheeks, our lips.
Now we're old, do you still think
of what could have been?
It's a shame, we were
so afraid to speak our minds at the time.

Failing is like a test

Failing is like a test.

It gives us a second chance to be our best.

To fail is part of life's destination and

what we learn from it we use as

motivation; dedication.

So, don't feel down if you fail,

for some things in life take a fail to make you

Prevail.

Just ordinary?

You have glitter in your veins and gold in your heart.

Your eyes are the stars that make the sky art.

And still you question if you're *just ordinary?*

Silent starry nights

People will say they are there for you when the sun is shining bright.

But a true friend is there for you even on the

silent

        starry

              nights.

Dear boys

Dear boys,
who told you that you shouldn't cry?
Who told you you're less of a man if you do?
You have a heart like us girls and you're human too.
And some things are hard to handle; to talk about;
to share,
but crying can be the way to show that you care.
So, do it boys and shed that tear or that
streaming waterfall you held in for a year.
Because,
Dear boys, you're human and humans cry
and no matter what your gender is,
it's perfectly fine.

Create yourself

Don't let the past define you.

You are you, to create.

Be your own best friend

Being let down; you get
used to it. The false
promises and excuses for
mistakes.
But there's only so much
you can take.
Put trust in yourself and be
your own best friend.

A heart of gold

I love too hard and I care too much but I'm not going to apologise for that. And I'm not going to give it up. There are plenty of people out there, in need of this type of attention. A hug to keep them warm. A shoulder to rest their head. I don't mind being there for them. At least I'll be able to see how my goodness has been spent. I've got so much to give to those in need; those who need. Maybe others should start to see that love is worth so much more than the material items they obsess over. A heart of gold is more valuable than you think. It pays the price of anything worthwhile.

Bed

Fresh white linen sheets and sunlight creeping in,
mint breeze and warm honey brushing at your
skin.

Best for you

I know I never got to say goodbye,
but I still hope the best for you.
I still want the best for you because you deserve it.
But most importantly,
I pray you'll see the best in you,
because you're worth it.

What happened to loyal friends?

What happened to loyal friends?
Is there such a thing?
The ones that stick by your side,
through the thick and thin.
And love you for you,
no matter what mood you're in.
It seems like some people don't have those kinds
of friendships.
The ones where they battle through storms and survive
without rips.
Loyalty just seems rare these days;
it's like you have to search.
So, for those of you with loyal friends,
be sure to treat them like merch.

*merch meaning merchandise

Natural state

Do you ever look at nature and think,

"What a beautiful thing!"?

The way the trees sway and the wind swirls and how
the birds sing.

It all seems like magic; as if too real to be.

The creatures, the sky, the ocean, the sea.

Harmony of music

I've tasted your soft melodies
and smelt your soothing harmonies.
I've rejoiced in your presence
and cherished all the memories.
And through the anxiety, sadness and
hopelessness,
you lullabied me back to hope.
You reside in my mind, melting me into a dream-
like state.
You live in my veins; my dependable drug.
Stitching my wounds together time after time.
My smile is caressed by your radiant rhythm.
Beat and bass matches the pounding of my heart.
A tranquillity of endless peace
is what you are when needed.
A breath of fresh air
is what you are when I need uplifting.
A place to fall in love
is what you'll always be to me.

Tired.of.this.

It's always me that makes the effort.
It's always me that tries.
It's always me trying to make you feel better.
It's gotten to the point where I wipe my own cries.
I'm.tired.of.this

Now we know what love is

You said that you loved us, but you hurt us.
And that stayed like a scar in our minds.
Every day of our lives.
But
we're stronger than that and now
we know what love is and how love should treat us.

Lessons in life

You'll never learn some lessons
until you make your mistakes.

Manipulation

Don't string me along or get me
twisted up in your mind games.
And don't use me and ditch me
like I'm just one of your targets or aims.
I have a heart, for a start.
And I'm not going to be a part
of your manipulation.

Old but youthful

Our bodies all get old.
But sometimes the youth is still in our minds;
digging up golden treasured memories;
the ones we thought we'd left behind.

Ready or not

Sometimes life chucks you into the deep end. You panic thinking that you can't swim but you forget that the rubber ring is right beside to keep you afloat; to stop you from drowning. And once you realise, you feel the calmness again and you remember just how precious life is. There are so many situations that we over analyse, thinking they're much worse than they actually are, or thinking that there's nobody there to help us along the way. We think if we haven't found ourselves by 21, we're a failure. If we haven't gone from school to university, we've done the educational path wrong. If we've never experienced the things in life that our friends have, then we are weird or not lucky enough. But I beg to differ. Life doesn't come with a rule book and even if it did, who would follow them anyway. Go and make something of yourself when you are ready. Whatever age that is. But also, be open to take opportunities that come your way, even when you are not ready; they could change you for the better.

What can a sprinkle of art do?

A sprinkle of Art
does magic to my heart.

Unsteady

I will never forget the way that I heard my heart
fall and crash to the ground that day.
I know I'm one of high expectations, but no one
told me it would hurt this bad. Wavering eyes
and wavering smiles.
I don't know where to look.
I don't know how to feel.
But one thing I know for certain is that
someday, I will heal.

A love game?

"Is this love, or is it a game?" I asked.
"Or are they both the same?" I asked.
"No, no, no." He laughed.
"In love, there can be two winners."

Blues

You remind me of the sky on hot days.
You remind me of the deep, deep ocean.
You remind me of the towel that I wrap my curls in.
You remind me of my tight skinny jeans.
You remind me of my school bag that I used to
swing close to my side.
You remind me of my very first car.
You remind me of the soulful music to my ears.
And you remind me of my first breakup.
But you remind me of happiness too.

Lucky to have you

How many shooting stars have you
forgotten to make a wish on?
And how many dreamcatchers do you
own?
How many times have you come across a
four-leaf clover?
How many fortune cats have caught your
eyes?
How many people have realised just how
rare you are?
But most importantly,
how many have told you just how lucky
they are to have you?

A part of their mind

At times, people will show us
parts of their minds.
And we'll be able see the best in them
when no one else could.
We will see a side that no one else would.
And we should really honour and cherish that because
there are people with minds
so guarded and locked that even they
can't free themselves.
For themselves.

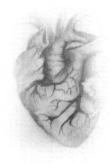

Dear heartbreak

Dear heartbreak,
why do you make my heart ache?
Why do you laugh at the teardrops
that stream down my face?
When I was in love, I was blind
and now you laugh at me as I try to find
the happiness I felt before.

I got you

At the end of the day, nobody really got your back
and they ain't going to cut you any slack,
when you need
to be freed,
from the problems you be facing
or the negative thoughts in your mind racing.
But I got you Boo
and we always
make it work.

Always heard

Often misunderstood.

Life's journey

Smile. Dream. Be happy.

Be happy. Dream. Smile.

Because life's a journey

and it only comes once.

So, you might as well complete the whole mile.

Till the end of time

Creativity flows from my veins like an
Indian waterfall from a cliff.
It's extraordinary.
Simply a part of me.
That I want to share with others.
Till the end of time.

Nowadays

Nowadays, everything is so quick…
Take a snap
Pose for the 'gram
We're all a victim of it.
We're caught up in a social life that isn't face to
face. We want to know who has the most
followers; it's like a game like a race.
It seems almost as if the simple things like talking,
meeting, and hanging out are a chore.
The oldies must think our generation is a bore.
But just because society expects us to act a certain
way, doesn't mean us young ones shouldn't get a
say. Yes, we are living in a technology-based era
but that doesn't mean that it will last forever.

Dreamers

Have you ever thought about what it's like up there
on the clouds?
They say I'm a kid for thinking thoughts like this
aloud.
Are they soft and fluffy like fairground candy
floss?
Are they just an illusion to our eyes?
Can they be held or not?
See, that's the thing about dreamers,
we think crazy thoughts a lot.

Secrets

Secrets are not a good thing,
I've heard.
For they can burden your life
and tear away at your soul.

The avoidable kill

Oh, I'm sorry if
watching your snaps
where I see you
killing yourself each day
hurts me.

Oh, I'm sorry if
I get upset seeing you
become such
a stranger;
a shadow of the person
you used to be.

Do you even remember the person
you used to be?
I wonder, do you even realise the hurt
you cause to people like me,
who see
you put yourself in danger like this?

You're a mess and you can see that.
Why did you have to let it get this far?
Why not let a friend in
to help de-stress your mind?
Not a fag, or weed, or any alcohol you can find!
The manipulating drugs
are not a friend who is kind.
This isn't a phase anymore,
it's your way of living.
Oh, I'm sorry if I can't stand by and
be complicit in your killing.

Hold my hand

I find comfort in the strength of your hands.
In the dark lines and creases of your sweet
palms.
The intricate finely sketched lines; faded but
still as strong as the bold ones.
The wrinkles around your knuckles.
The delicacy of your skin.
The same hands that guided me
through this rollercoaster of a life.
Time and time again.

Just like my bedroom

I am complex.

Just like my bedroom…

You will trip and fall over socks, jeans, and books
just to get to my wardrobe.
The same way that you will trip and fall,
trying to understand the way to get to the
depths of my heart.

Beauty (n.)

Every little thing about you.

I'm trying to work it out

You ask a lot of me.
I don't know if that's good
because that means you must
think that I'm loyal.
                    Or bad, because that means that you must
                            think you can use me?
                        I won't tire myself out trying to work
                                    it out.
                But I just hope that it's the first one.

White noise

When I talk
they all talk
over me.
And when they talk
I listen.
It's a shame really.
I am full of
such wonderful ideas.
Maybe I'll learn
to share them with
open minds as delicate as my own.

Hurdles

Bella, she said, *"Why would you want to run with
something in your way?"*
And I said, *"Maybe to show you can get over it?"*
Skye, she said, *"I can't jump over it!"*
And I said, *"That's your homework; your worst
enemy
if you have any; everything you hate, now jump!"*
Maybe at the time I didn't realise that I was
referencing life.
There are so many obstacles that you will face,
but it's
how you overcome them that makes you strong;
that makes you realise that in life
sometimes the inconveniences are what keep you
going.
So next time you approach a hard time,
think how much stronger you'll be once you're
over it, once you've gotten through it, once it's all
behind you.
Doesn't that bring a smile to your face?

I value you

People let me down so
much.
It's become regular.
But you guys don't so, I've
got to give credit
to ya.

Jigsaw

There are some things
that you don't even
have to let go of.
They just
fall apart by themselves
because they were never
meant to be connected to you.
Never meant to be.
Just like you can't force
two jigsaw pieces together
and expect a masterpiece.

Friends

Stay away from those that love to manipulate.
Full of disrespect and hate.
Only want to talk with you in the absence of their mate.

What will be, will be

What will be, will be.

I'm wishing the best for you and me.

Hoping our love is like a fairy tale;

Never ending happy endings.

Qué sera, sera

Qué sera sera.

Estoy deseando lo major para tu y para mí.

Esperar que nuestro amor sea como un cuento de hadas;

Con un final feliz.

How to live

Learn to live.
Take those risks.
And step out of your comfort zone.
You can always learn that much more
when you're with others and not alone.

You and I

Some things are just meant to be.
I hope one of those things is us.

A better destination

I'm moving on to
better things;
better journeys
and better places.
Places where you can't tear me down
or break me into
p i e c e s

The world is truly beautiful

I know that we humans aren't perfect. But that still
doesn't explain why we haven't learned yet. From
our mistakes and our hate. All the shootings,
killings, and bombs.

It's like what's the point in learning from history,
if us humans keep repeating his story? And what's
the point in learning from the past, when we just
move in circles and end up where we were last?
They say it takes one person to stand up and make
a change and maybe that's true. And it's sad
because *the world is truly beautiful;*

It seems us humans just fill it with pure evil.

The flower garden

Promise me that if you find me again,
you'll put colour in my life,
like the flowers in the garden.
And promise me that this time,
you'll watch me bloom.

Another place

People think mainly of two places here;
Earth and space.
But
when I kiss you, I discover another.

Satisfied

I can prosper in any situation.
Alone.
Or with others.
Because I do not cling to the
negative and I do not cling
to what I want things to be like.
I live in the moment.
I indulge in the happiness.
I delight in the content of my self being.
I do not let ideas, situations,
or people determine my worth.
I always remember that being
satisfied with my life begins with
being satisfied with my own self.

Learn how to fly

In life, there are strange people who think they
have control over you. They think they own you,
but they don't. They think you'll stay trapped
with them, but you won't. Because
one day you'll learn how to *fly.*

The school system

I remember when school
tried to tell me that
I had to change my shoes.
"Plain black." They said
"No heel, no bow."
What did they think I wanted to do?
Turn up for school like I was at a fashion show?
It's funny,
they tried to act like the way I dressed
would affect my education.
But if anything,
it was the school that needed close inspection.
And I've never experienced prison
but I experienced school
and isn't that close enough?
The curriculum was so restricted
that thinking outside of the box became tough.

They taught me the basics
but when I had days off and travelled
I learned so much more stuff.
They told me to accept others
and to show respect.
But I think that's just hypocrisy at its best,
when you've got kids in 'bottom set'
not getting the help they need
being labelled, 'bad'
when they're bright
and just want to be freed
from the stereotype.

And the teachers taught me a lot of different subjects,
I'll be honest.
Like Maths, English, Science
and when it came to homework,
I was always working on it.
But what about learning how to pay the bills, manage
money?
I'm not being funny
but what about politics too?
what about history that isn't all about World War II?
What about worldly matters?
I'm sure if they taught us this
then less kids would be in tatters,
gangs and feelings hopeless –
wanting to hope less
for their futures.
And I know it's a two-way thing,
kind of like a relationship.
But how can the kids ask for help
when the school system
is sinking like a ship.

I remember when school
locked me in a building
and confined me.
Four walls
some chairs
a table and a whiteboard.
A break and lunchtime where I feel the fresh breeze
and see my friends

isn't going to prepare me for the real world
they keep me away from.
And when my mom would ask me how my
school day went
I'd say, "It was alright."
While holding in the words,
"Changes need to be made,
more than a few,
more than some.
Mama, they need to teach us the facts of life."

Your eyes are the stars

They say the eyes are the key to the soul.
But what if your eyes are the stars?
How beautiful your soul must be!

Just one person

Funny how one person can mean so much to you,
without them even knowing that they do.
It's funny that they can be the reason for your
smiles,
and the reason your worries find a place to hide.
Isn't it funny how just one person can make you
feel at home,
when you're struggling and feeling all alone?

Destined for great things

Soak your mind and soul in
sweet smelling bath salts.
Cleanse all the toxic and negative vibes.
Then remind yourself
that nobody should treat you
like you are unworthy of being loved.
Tell yourself that you are destined for great things.

Let's find ourselves

It's all a rush

It's all a blur

Everything happening too fast, all at once

But for once,

Let us find time to find ourselves.

Stop worrying

Let's stop worrying about the problems that we can't
solve.
Let's stop worrying about the issues we think we
can't resolve.
Let's stop worrying about the people that don't care
about us.
Let's stop worrying that we need to change ourselves
or adjust.
Let's stop worrying that maybe we're not good
enough.
Let's stop worrying that coming out of our comfort
zone might be tough.
Let's stop worrying about the things we can't control.
Let's stop worrying that we won't be able to get out
of this
black hole of
worry that
stops us from thinking that we're not worth it.

Dear aesthetics

Dear aesthetics, and to those who see the beauty in everything.

Thank you for keeping the camera of your eye open and capturing the beauty of life.

Victimisation

You do not have to stay
in a situation that makes
your heart ache with pain
or your eyes stream with tears
or your mind overthink the minute details.

You do not have to stay
in a situation that kills you inside
day and night and
strips you of your
own identity.

You do not need to let them have power over you
that was not rightfully theirs to have in the first
place.

Important feet -ure of my life

You keep me walking.
You keep me running.
You keep me dancing.

You keep me pedalling.
You keep me stomping.
You keep me spinning.

You keep me standing
and that is why you will always be
an important feet-ure of my life
even if I do take you for granted.

The next chapter of your life

The next chapter of your life doesn't have to start

at new year or Christmas or tomorrow.

It can begin tonight or right now as you

thank the Lord for the fresh breath of air

he gave you today.

That's the kind of chapter that will have you optimistic

for the next

Chapter too.

Be yourself with me

I know you guard your emotions.
You laugh when you want to cry.
And you smile and say, "it's okay"
when you know that it's a lie,
but it really is okay;
you can be yourself with me.

The hurting heart

Hurting hearts do the most crying.
Then the tears flow through the pen into writing a
poem of their thoughts.

The caring friend

I have many friends, yet I'm still in a group by myself.
I look out for every one of my friends.

Sometimes I try to solve your problems first while I put
mine on a shelf.
I care, and I try to give the best advice when you ask,
even though I may be juggling other things; trying to
multitask.
Before, I would think that you were trying to be like
me and I'm a firm believer in being you.
but what I couldn't believe is that I was the person who
helped you to find yourself.

I will always be there for you when you need a friend;
when you have a load of questions that have no end.
And when you need a hand to hold,
I'll be the one you cling onto,
with an ear always open for you for your troubles,
and all your worries.

Smile for the future

Smile for the future.
For the things you have yet to accomplish
and the things you have yet to overcome.
Smile for the future, and the new you,
you have yet to become.

The ambition in you

I've got faith in you.
and in every little thing that you do.
Your eyes; they are fierce like the fiery orange sunset;
blinding those in your sight.
You pave the path you wish to walk in,
in luminous gold light.
And some are jealous, sickly green, ill and bitter;
passing their hate onto others like a transmitter.
But the ambition in your eyes is more than enough to
set them alight;
to block out the unnecessary with all your might,
to shine and to dazzle like the shooting fireworks in
the night.
I've got faith in you.
and in every little thing that you do because
in every little thing that you do you have faith.
And you have ambition.

Only half of themselves

Sometimes people only show you half of themselves.
Sometimes they only give you half of themselves.
Half of their loving,
half of their soul,
half of their care,
as if their heart is empty like a hole.
But they expect everything you have in return; your all.
But I guarantee that they'll be the ones
who won't catch you when you fall.

Water of life

More than a liquid.
    A lifeline.
Light blue like the sky,
or transparent. Pure.
                Her name is water.
She lives as a lake, by the hillside in the countryside.
There she is neither blue or pure but brown. Dark
brown and murky, rippling with thick dirt.
Contrasting the glorious fresh blanket of sky above.
She flows down deep and deeper into a river.
Pollution flows through and around her; fishes dying
around her as the soil chokes their gills.

And then the ocean. She can transform into one of
those too.
Vast; almost as if she has no end.
This is when she is most beautiful. Glistening azure,
rippling gracefully, finally reflecting the pureness of
the sky above while boats sail within her across her
surfs.

She lives in a tap, both hot and cold, streaming out in
currents each and every morning. Splashing,
gushing, filling up like she has a never-ending
supply. Overflowing from time to time but she drips
lonely and daily.

Renewed and recycled.
In a bottle, she lives.
Encased in plastic, with a logo and a cap to keep her
contained.
In this form, she is easily obtained;
In all seasons and all weathers, summer, spring,
autumn, winter. Every second,
every minute,
every hour,
every day.
So easily accessible in every kind of way.
We can cleanse ourselves of our daily struggles and
start afresh the next day.

But in another place, another land, another world, she
does not exist in this way or in this form. Here, she
lives in dreams and desperate cries.
Cries that wait exhaustingly for her arrival onto their
starved parched cracking dark lips.
She is more than a liquid.
        She's a lifeline.
But why can't she save them?

Water of life: Alternative version

There are people who need it,
people who want it,
people who have it but still waste it.
It's strong enough to save your life
and strong enough to take it away.
Such a beautifully elegant aspect of nature.
Such an important element of life to appreciate;
to be thankful for.
Let that sink in.
Drown you sorrows,
this is larger than life itself.

Moonlight performer

No one asks the moon if he's afraid of the dark.
We just assume he creates his own spotlight
in the night sky
and owns the stage.

Goodbye

I never understood when people used to
say, 'see you later' instead of 'goodbye.'
They said it hurts a little less.
They said it sounds a little less final.
Then tell me where my tears went when
you walked and never came back without
saying a single word goodbye.

The "better" friends

The friends that are there for you in the good.

They're good.

But those friends that stay with you through the bad, aren't bad;

They're better.

Drowning

I've drowned enough times in my own tears.
Now, it's time to dry my eyes because I don't
carry my burdens in boats anymore.

Good things take time

There was a part of me that
envied you and
I know that I shouldn't feel like that.
I know better things will come
my way when
I am ready for them and I know
that good things take time.

The best gift for yourself

Your heart has looked after you
and loved you
from the start of time.
So, the best kind of love
you could possibly
give to yourself is self-love.
That's the best gift
you could ever ask from yourself.
Wrap it up in a box with a ribbon.
Label it 'Handle with care.'

The truth is

Do you remember when
I said I didn't care?
Well the truth is
I never stopped caring at all.
And do you remember how I never opened up to you or
told you how I really felt.
Well the truth is
I was scared of giving my all.

Your talent

See, you're the one I think about when my body jolts awake in the morning. And during the day when events don't go the way I planned them. Or when I think my day could not have gone any better. And you're always the one that I think about when my sleepless brain won't switch off at night. And what's funny is that one person may have read this thinking I was talking about a person, a lover, a friend, an admirer. And you wouldn't be wrong.

But another person, may have read and understood that I was talking about a goal, a gift, a passion that won't leave you. A talent that is as much a part of you as the skin you are wearing.

You will understand that if you ever feel like this about something that you enjoy, then you have truly found your calling in life. You have found what you love. Don't let it go. Grasp it tightly because this talent is as much a part of you as the air that you breathe and without it... well, we all know what would happen.

The backpack

I got rid of that backpack of guilt I was carrying around
with me. I dropped it off somewhere where no one could
find it; where no one could see.
Somewhere desolate and isolated.
Far away from me.
And I don't intend to get it back.
My back is free from pain.
And I never thought that I would feel like that again.
Now there's nothing weighing down my shoulders.
No negativity or boulders of guilt that there was before.
I'm finally free. I'm finally me.

Let our voices be heard

I'm really, really angry and I'll tell you why.
I'm angry at the world's injustice and
I'm angry with the medias lies.
When I try to help those in need,
I give to the growing charities,
but it seems it's never enough, it's such a rarity.
Because every time I look,
it's always the same people suffering,
So I'm deeply confused as to what's
happening to the money I am offering.
I really want to know where it is travelling,
I really want to know where it is going.

And I'm angry about the hatred
that people have for other people
and how they think that they should not be equal
just because they're too dark, from another country,
or speak another language.
Young girls and women are treated like an object,
and people just sit back and try to ignore the subject.
I hate how some celebrities think
they're a better person than us,
just because they're in the limelight
and earn more money than us.

I'm angry at the corrupt world we live in,
where the goodhearted people are dying
and the cruel and malicious are living.
But what makes me most angry
is there is nothing that I can do.
These types of problems are not something
that one person can fix alone.
But if you agree with
what I'm saying then let's come together,
to let these matters be known.
Let our voices be heard!

Weather

When it's winter and the earth is encased
in a white frosted wonderland,
we crunch through it,
we leave footprints,
we make snow angels,
we have snowball fights,
but we optimistically wait for summer.
And when it's summer,
we wear less,
we suck ices,
we have a family BBQ
and we wander bare footed in the sand.
We drench ourselves in cold water when we complain
it's too hot; furtively wishing it was cooler.

The diary

I tell you about my day and all the ups and the
downs that I've had.

I tell you about the things that make me happy
and the things that make me sad.

I tell you all my secrets because I know you'll
keep them safe.

Sometimes I wonder about all the secrets that I've
told you over the years; and how many smiles
you caught and how many tears.

But I know that you'll always be there.

And I'm sure you'll always care.

Dear diary, thank you.

Being inspired

Learning new things every day and creating
ideas in each and every way.
Now that's being inspired at its finest.

Distance apart but still close by

We're under the same sky yet we're a distance
apart.
Our skin is yet to touch but the love is in our
heart.
It's funny how little distance means,
when someone means so much.
It's not virtual, it's entirely real and it makes me
feel such
Happiness and Joy
Wow, how that can take over your life
when you least expect it!
I never searched to find it.
This blessing, this connection, it doesn't feel like
any other.
Yes, we're a distance apart but still under the
same sky
But this connection is so real, it seems as if
you're close by.

Recovery

Hard times can leave wounds from your past.
And maybe one day,
someone will want to read them.
But by then,
you'll have scars that tell a thousand stories
of your present.
And it will be you who reads them aloud.

Don't break my heart

The way you got me feeling has really
got me believing
That I ain't hard to love and you
ain't ever leaving.
But this love best be real because
I don't want to deal
with the disease of a "broken heart" -
the one they talk of in the movies.

The book of your life

Some people will ruin a chapter of your life
and hold on to see the ending of your book.
But what they fail to understand is that
each chapter is a sequel and
not everyone gets to look.

A new me

I woke up, looked in the mirror, and saw a smile on my face.

I saw a light in my eyes and I felt strength in my bones.
And I remembered all the times I almost gave up on my hopes and dreams.

What a joke.
Look at me now.
Look at how,
I seize the day, not with both hands, but with my whole being.

I laugh, and I sing because I'm a free spirit.
No one said it was going to be easy, but I took the risk anyway.

You've got to be open to make changes,
to see the changes and that's what I did.
Now, I can believe in myself and believe in all the things I can achieve.

Now I can look to the future and be ready to take the paths that may not be easy.

Now I can see in myself, the person I worked so hard to be.

The words of art

Give me a letter.
Give me a word.
Give me a phrase and
let me manipulate
the words of art that buzz
through my brain,
faster than a lightning
bolt.

Just freedom at its finest

Like an angel or a goddess or a queen or a king;
stripped of their duties but not denied of their
beauties.
Free and untamed from life itself,
free and untamed from the rituals and failures it
brings;
free like the whistling winds and breeze or like the
tune of the small sparrow when it sings.
Free like a warm embrace from a loved one
or a smile, laughter, love and happiness.
Just freedom at its finest.
That's what we all crave isn't it?

I found a lover

It's so strange.
It's like
I found a friend in you,
then a best friend in you
and I loved you through it all.
You're the best thing that
I never even dreamed I'd meet
but I'm so glad I did.
I'm so glad and I'm so grateful
and you must be mad
to not stay in my life forever.
I found a lover in you.
Please stay.

Recollected memories

Sweet jasmine scented milk,
skin as smooth as soft silk,
dark honey coloured eyes,
tear stained windows
and tear stained skies.
Happy smiles constructed from the heart,
intricate written letters; a work of art,
warm sunny clear days,
recollected memories of joy.

Magic

One day I realised that there was magic in the world,
and not the kind that you see magicians do
because the magic was simply you.
You came into my life like an angel,
picked out the gems of my soul
and showed me,
so that I'd learn to appreciate
my inner beauty.
You taught me that I was made from the same
vivacity as the stars in the dusky nocturnal sky,
and that I shouldn't be afraid of the roasting fire in
my eyes because that was my strength.
You told me that the sweet elaborate words that I
kept locked away in the box of my mind could be
freely spoken and that I was truly extraordinary.
And for this, I'll always be thankful that you came into
my life and made me believe in magic.
Because now I realise that there is really magic in this
world; not the kind that you see magicians do,
But the kind that is simply me.

If you really care

If you really care, you'll try to make an effort.
You'll never give me a reason to question.
You'll treasure our memories till the end of time;
The good and the bad, the ones that are old
but still sparkle and shine.
You'll act on your spoken words.

If you really care, you'll try to make an effort.
You'll not fire excuses
to why we haven't talked in a while
or blame it on the fact that we live more than a mile
apart.
If you really care, you'll show it,
in whichever way you can.
You'll show it through your actions.
Surely, that's not too much to ask.

Treasure

Treasure me like a locket.
Keep me safe in the depths of your pocket.
So, when I'm lonely or in despair,
I'll know that I'm still
Loved.

Time out for yourself

It's okay to take some time out for yourself;
to revisit the fresh roses in your mind
and free them of their thorns. It's okay.
Take time to water them and watch them grow more,
till they are the most beautiful roses you've ever seen.

They don't love you now

They don't love you now, but they will do in the future,
when you're bigger than they imagined you'd be.
And bigger than they want you to be.
And then they'll say you're blocking their view to see.
But even if they do, keep going.
Become who you said you always wanted to be.

Honey

Two round pots of honey; sweet like your sugar-coated heart.

I wouldn't want to turn you bitter.

Outshine the sun

Those who go through life sprinkling positive vibes
on everyone like fairy dust, deserve the most
love and gratitude.
Those who go through life sprinkling a little hope
to those who grieve; thank you for keeping
the uplifting attitude.
The shines of smiles that you bring to peoples' faces
must surely be enough to outshine the sun.

Falling in love with everything

We live our lives falling in love with

other people's appearance

other people's style,

other people's personalities,

other people's ideas.

But what about learning

to fall in love with ourselves.

Dazzle the stars

Your laugh can dazzle the stars,
almost as if without you,
they'd be nothing special.

My friends are gems

Here I was sat, thinking that I was losing my friends
when really, I was losing myself.
I was focusing on myself
and I put everything else on a shelf.
And when I was struggling, no one was there to help,
but I never reached out in the first place.

I was oblivious to the people whom I needed
and to them that needed me too.
And for that, I am sorry.
Sorry to myself and to you, for thinking
you didn't care like I did for you.
Funny how stages in your life can affect you,
but thank you for staying by my side,
all the way through.
All of you.
You are gems; rare but true.

Moving on

If I'm moving on
without you then
you were too slow,
keeping up.

Singing sweet in heaven

I miss you.
I miss your laugh.
I miss your cuddles.
I miss your warmth.
I miss your kisses.
I miss your voice.
I miss your singing.
I miss you
and the love that I miss out on
when you're not home.
I hope you're still
singing sweet in heaven.

Make a poem from these random words

Written at the Storysmash event: Panya Banjoko's Poetry Masterclass. 23rd February 2018.

Healing;
intelligently cooler in the summer,
there's a huge ton of good for you
and your future,
not to miss perfect living space pays off.
Join us for another record year.

A reckless thunderstorm

You are my sunshine,
but on rainy days,
I do not search for your light
as I know you can be
a reckless thunderstorm too.

The black boy

He's got brown eyes.
The kind of eyes that go unnoticed.
The kind of eyes that are forgotten to be termed 'beautiful'.
But no one sees when they melt
like sweet honey in the sunlight.
No one sees when they look hazel. He's got a
gentle heart too, one that you wouldn't want to break;
one that is so ready to give.
A gentle heart that needs to be
guarded with subtle hands.
He's got the darkest complexion to the human eyes.
Dark but rich, like the night minus the stars,
minus the moon
and minus the lights of the houses.
But it's a shame it's only the colour of his skin
that they noticed first.
It's a shame that the colour of his skin could not go
unnoticed to their eyes.
For a good heart,
a good soul,
can show on the surface,
if only you look beyond your own perceptions.
If only you look close enough.

People who need to be cherished

They say you must learn to love yourself before
you can even love anyone else.
But tell me how there are people that can love others so
much more than they can even love themselves, pour
their most delicate advice into others than into
themselves,
give the most praise and affection to others than to
themselves.
These are the most underestimated people who need to be
cherished. Always.

To sleep

Trying to sleep last night was a myth.

But thinking of you was legendary.

Isn't God clever?

Some people are artists.
Some people are the art themselves.

And there are some people out there that are both.

Isn't God clever?

Better days

I had so many ups and downs.
I almost lost myself along the way.
I fell down a deep black hole
and then I rescued myself and saw the light in the day.
I appreciated it's beauty
and prayed that there would be better days.
Just like this.
For I know what it's like to fall
but I know what it's like to walk again.

Limbo state

I wish that I could tell you
the hidden words written on my lips.
The words that have been produced from deep within;
from my heart.
But maybe I'm not good enough.
Maybe I'm not good enough for you.

They tell me not to give my all
but what do I do when I give my love so easily.
I wish that I could share how I feel,
without feeling like I've given you all the stars in the sky
when you just want the moon from someone else. I think
maybe I'm not good enough.
Maybe I'm not good enough for you.

I wish that I could tell you
the hidden words written on my lips.
And pour out my heart.
And stop thinking that I'm not good enough for you.
Take me out of this limbo state.
I am more than good enough for you.

There are people here for you

There are always people here for you,
who care for you, who will walk the hard road with you.
There are people here for you who will listen to you
even if they are not able to change how you feel.
A pair of ears can do so much for your fears.
And before long the flowers will be blooming,
the sun will be rising
and you will realise that life
is too beautiful to not live again.

What's holding you back?

What's holding you back?
Nothing
but yourself.
Go and capture the world
and make it yours!

Reminds me of an angel

You remind me of an angel
who experiences
the pain of the world
yet continues to emit
such gentleness,
such love,
such warmth.
Tell me how you do it each day?

A switch of focus

Some will call it 'selfish'
but we all need some time for ourselves.
Sometime where we can learn
to appreciate ourselves
and the body that keeps us alive
doing such wonderful things each day.
Breathing,
blinking,
our hearts beating.
Some will call it 'selfish'
but it's just a switch of focus from others to ourselves.
If only for a day.

Someday, somehow

You shouldn't dwell
on who or what hurt you.
I find it so sad that you
blame your past for the
decisions that you make now.
I hope you'll be alright,
I hope you'll return to the old you
someday, somehow.

The naturist

Skin naked.
Green speckled eyes.
Freckles.
A daffodil flower tattoo on the ankle.
Vinyl playing Sabrina Claudio.
Sun peeking through the window pane.
Polaroid pictures.
A free spirit,
no care, no shame.

Go and lose your mind

You'll drive yourself mad
thinking about people who
don't even care about you.
They're driving themselves happy
moving on.
Maybe you should try that too.
Go lose your mind on things that matter.

Winter baby

I stick my tongue out and catch the snowflakes.
My eyes twinkle to match the glistening of the
cold frost, I rub my hands together and stick them
into my pockets.
I make fresh footprints; hearing the crunch of the
frozen sheet beneath me.
I smile; my teeth as white as the ice. We hold
hands, as the white sheet floods arounds us;
winter baby.

You are stronger than you think

You have a heart that is strong, sturdy, stout.
One that fights back like a soldier in knight's armour,
and like a shield, it protects you.
Protects you from the malicious words of others.
But at times, you doubted it.
You doubted the heart you had and it strengths;
the fights it fought,
the love it offered,
and this meant
that when people wounded you,
you felt your heart crack; fragment,
and fall to pieces.
And you cried,
wiped your tears,
and tried
to pick yourself back up, but your heart,
it put its pieces back together, by itself.
It recovered.
And that was when you learned
that you were stronger than you thought.

J for Jake

Four years old.
Big dog.
Dark brown but you look black.
Energetic.
Big brown happy eyes.
I hide.
I'm scared.
Your bark is very loud.
Sometimes you bark when I'm at the door.
You run very fast.
I dropped chocolate bars once.
You ate them. Oops.
You sniff my leg.

Seventeen years old.
You're not so big anymore.
But your coat is still so gorgeous and new.
You barely move; slumped down on the rug.
You stare at me with those glossy tear-stained dark eyes,
like you're sad.
You're in pain.
Tears prick my eyes.
You're tired.
And you're slow.
And there's nothing that I can do.

Then I'm crying.
Praying that you'll be okay.

They said you only have a few more weeks.
Wednesday.
I was going to come and see you.
The tears are there again.
But not in your eyes; in mine.

Four years old.
Big dog.
First dog I ever loved.
J for Jake.

Creative minds

Go and connect with
creative minds.
They'll show you another world
you've never seen before.
They'll make you see beauty
in places you expected
destruction.

Needle and thread

You're so unsure of yourself that you keep others on a
thread around you.
Dangle them carelessly to the side.
Pull them nearer when needed.
You wrap others in endless knots and ties and tangles
when your mind is in a twist itself.
But you have to learn that you're a needle
and they are a thread.
Maybe sometime in the future,
you'll realise that you will need them
to help you
pull yourself together.

The sun and the blossom

The sun - he keeps me warm,
makes me happy,
helps me grow.
The sun - he helps me spring
into life and lets me know, that
I am beautiful.
Beautifully placed upon this earth.
I represent life, death, and rebirth.

You are not superhuman

You can't help everyone.
You can't save everyone.
And you can't be everything to everyone.
Even though you think you can.
You'll drain yourself out.
Every ounce of golden glitter
that sprinkles from your heart,
don't let it go to waste.

Don't let it go to matters that you won't be able to escape.
See, you are unique and special
and maybe that's why you attract the broken hearted,
the pessimistic and the lonely.
 But when you're feeling down and blue,
there is no one around to care for you.
Nobody to give you words of wisdom
or offer a hand to cling to.

You have to learn to let go, so that you can be free,
because you are not superhuman,
no matter how hard you try to be.

The only person I trust

Have you ever felt so hurt
that you lost the trust in others?
Yes, me too.
But I mended myself
and now I'm fixed.
It's all just a thing of the past.
These things never last.
But now the only person I trust
is
myself.

Mankind

Why can't we learn to love others for who they are?
For the mother that she is,
for the pure joyous boy that he is,
for the gifted girl that she is,
for the loving grandad that he is going to be.
Our eyes,
they may not be our own creation
but they were sculptured and designed by the same
creator;
our innovator.
Our skin,
whether dark like the night,
honey roasted
or untainted white
should be loved,
should be appreciated,
should be admired.
For who we are
and what we look like
and how we express,
all tell a fascinating story of our history and digress into
this world
that sometimes lacks the meaning of happiness.
Sweet lips of a man or a woman, but how comes so much
hatred pours out?

Hatred that is gooey, black,
and green and mean.
Hatred that grows on prejudice, discrimination, and
racism it seems does not remind us of the beauty deep
within us.
The beauty in our souls; it is the equivalent of a lightly lit
tunnel
leading us to the place we call home;
away from abhorrence and trouble.
It leads us to a place of our roots, like a delicate
blossoming flower in the soil
and reminds us that love is within us all.

11:11 – The wishing hour

I wish for good health,
a better self,
a lot of success,
a chance to be my best,
an abundance of blessings,
hardships with happy endings.

Betrayal

I told you I didn't want to be forgotten
and when I came back, the first four words
from your mouth were not "I love you too." but
"Knock knock, who's there?"
I said, "It's not a joke, stop playing."
And you said, "I'm not playing either."

Chances

Chance after chance is
what I give.
A promise that can't be broken is
what I need.

Empty talk

"Have a good day!" They said
but it was just a figure of speech.
"We'll keep in touch!" They said
and then they stopped making an effort.
"I'm here if you need me!" They said
but when I looked they were nowhere to be found.
"I always have time for you!" They said
but by then it was too late.

Like a lion

Your exterior is strong and fearless
but we know inside
that you're far from heartless.

Babe

Do you call me 'Babe'
to decorate our conversations?
Or do you call me 'Babe'
because you see a 'Queen' in
me?

No labels

I've learned
to stop putting labels onto people.
I've learned not to expect certain things from certain
people just because of the pointless name I give them.
(Friend, Best friend, Girlfriend,
Boyfriend, Cousin, Auntie, Uncle)

Because sometimes you realise that those
you thought were your real friends
are actually your enemies,
only waiting for your down fall.
And sometimes you realise that those
you thought were family
are quick to disown you when
there are slight misunderstandings.

So, from now on, if you're there for me,
if you care for me,
if you can forgive me when I'm in the wrong,
if you can make an effort to be there,
without me having to ask then,
I love you
and that is the only label you need.

Home

All we ever do is search
for a place to call our home.
Whether it be a place,
an emotion,
a person or an object.
And that's what makes us human.
That's that makes us feel
a sense of belonging.

Her Karma

I looked back at my old self and I said
"Why did you hold on for so long?
"Why did you let him treat you that way?"
"Why couldn't you see the truth?"
"Why were you so blind to who he really was?"
And then I turned all the questions around
And I said
"Why did he hold on for so long?"
"Why did he let me treat him that way?"
"Why couldn't he see the truth?"
"Why was he so blind to see who I really was?"
And I replied
"Because boys don't realise a real goddess until she's gone."
I smiled.
Now he's running back, saying he really cares for me.
But I'm living in the present now, and I'm still treading
carefully, hoping that the past is kept in the past.
So, I turn to say to him, "Sorry, who are you? Who are
you?"
And Karma, she laughs
and laughs with me too.

His Karma

I looked back at my old self and I said
"Why did you hold on for so long?
"Why did you let her treat you that way?"
"Why couldn't you see the truth?"
"Why were you so blind to who she really was?"
And then I turned all the questions around
And I said
"Why did she hold on for so long?"
"Why did she let me treat her that way?"
"Why couldn't she see the truth?"
"Why was she so blind to see who I really was?"
And I replied
"Because girls don't realise a real god until he's gone."
I smiled.
Now she's running back, saying she really cares for me.
But I'm living in the present now, and I'm still treading
carefully, hoping that the past is kept in the past.
So, I turn to say to her, "Sorry, who are you? Who are
you?"
And Karma, he laughs
and laughs with me too.

Like a rose

You're pure hearted. You just want the simple things in life. And there's nothing wrong with that. You just want the best for everybody. You fall in love so easily because you can't help but see the beauty in everything. In all the things in the world. And there's nothing wrong with that either. People will question you and ask why you are the way you are. They will question if you're genuine. But you won't need to explain. How will they possibly understand that to you, everyone is as stunning as the stars shining in the pitch-black sky? How will they understand why you still treat those that broke your heart like precious diamonds because you don't want theirs cracked either? How will they understand why you try to make everyone smile because you like the way their eyes smile and sparkle like jewels? They wouldn't understand. And that's okay. Because one day someone will, and they will tell you that you're pure hearted. Like a rose.

And aren't roses the most beautiful?

Optimism

My darling, why do you marvel
at the thunderstorms,
at the fire, at the hatred, at death?
When, my darling,
you have an entire universe
waiting for you.

Young days

I miss the young days, the free days,
the content days.
The days where the breeze was cool and
I would fly a red kite into the sky
with my father by my side,
singing birds passing by.
I miss catching butterflies in the summer,
running from bees
and chasing pigeons
and devouring ice creams in the heat;
it was a treat
for the day.
The sickly-sweet vanilla, sticky on my lips, on
my cheeks and on my hands.

Riding my bike with my friends, grubby
hands of mud from the falling over we had done.
Stained jeans with grass,
stained faces with joy
until it was time to go home
where the sibling rivalry would begin.
And for dinner, we'd have rice and chicken.
I miss the young days,
the free days,
the content days.
Not that these days aren't good anymore.
They're just not the same.

Inner reflection

It's a shame
how he searched
for love
so badly each day
that when it stared
at him in the
mirror each day
he couldn't see it.

Him

I'm grateful,
I'm thankful,
I'm blessed
to have life.
Bad days are like hell; seeming like a never-
ending pit of dread and like a fiery temper,
sizzling and rising like lava.
But the best days are like heaven compared.
And these are the days I pray for;
breathe for.
Sweet, precious, breathtakingly bright days,
doves cooing in harmony.
Nothing negative could ever dim the light.
God by my side.
Love in my heart.
I'm learning to be an angel;
to see the good in others regularly, think good
thoughts daily.
Pessimism is becoming a rarity.
I'm learning how to spread an aura of forgiving
dust onto others every time I can because
I am made of clay from the earths ground,
moulded, sculptured, and designed, all from the
mud.

But who I live to be and the things I live to do,
is to please the greatest, the highest, by doing good.
I'm learning to be the best me every day, trying to
reconnect with the faith,
because I'm grateful,
I'm thankful,
I'm blessed,
to have life.
So, I'm going to make it the best it can
be. He knows, He sees,
He believes in me.
For I am a mere puppet in this world,
I am a fish among others learning to swim,
I am a flower among the many blossoming blooms in the
garden,
I am a person among the many other people in the
world.
But I am learning, most importantly to be a lamb
and to follow him, each day.

Watch the sunset with me

Watch the sunset with me. Forget about your troubles and watch the colours of the sky, while other people let their world flitter by.

My tranquillity

Sleep is my tranquillity
and my sanctuary
when I'm feeling low
and raggedy.
Sleep is my tranquillity
like a medicine prescribed
for me to keep my sanity.
When sticks and stones break my bones,
sleep never fails to repair me.
It refreshes my mind and brings
me back to long forgotten memories.
It's like a sweet kind of remedy that
helps me to forget my pain and my troubles.
Nightmares or nice dreams,
it is still my tranquillity.
Sleep is such a beautiful state,
which I love to experience
over and over again.
Because, honestly, without it,
I think I would truly go insane.

I am so proud of you

I know that you are going to go onto
better things and achieve such amazing things.
I never doubt that.
I know that you will make such a greater version of
yourself.
Such a new transformation that you'll laugh at the
smashed mirror containing your old reflection.
You are so capable;
capable of such creativity and your energy
and your soul is just enough to cure
others of their blindness and vulnerability.
You are amazing.
But please do remember that once
you were like a locked treasure box;
rusty, abandoned, and old,
until you were smashed open
to reveal all your jewels and gold.
You were once like a precious lily;
parched and bowing to the ground,
but once watered and fed,
you bloomed prettier than the other flowers around.

Please don't forget where you started and
what you had,
what you went through and
who helped you,
get to where you are now.
And if you can remember that, you'll always understand
why
I look upon your face with such wonder,
such amazement and such awe.
You are amazing.
Never forget that.
Please, don't ever forget that
I am so proud of you.

Becoming ourselves again

We don't talk anymore.
But that's alright.
I managed to forgive you for the times you hurt me
without it ending in a fight.
But I won't forget the way you treated me, because see,
everything happens for a reason.
And sometimes we don't realise in the moment,
that the pain we feel in our hearts,
is only just the start,
of us becoming ourselves again.

A for appreciation

Appreciation. Even the word is under-appreciated. Tell me. What does appreciation mean to you? Does a particular person come to mind? Let's start with the people that love you for you. Who stay by your side and always pray that you will showcase the best version of yourself to the world. And those who still ride this rollercoaster called, 'Life' with you on your worst days. I'm talking about our mothers, fathers, siblings, cousins, aunts and uncles, friends, best friends, partners. Even strangers. The ones who smile politely at you in the street. And although this may sound odd, but let's appreciate all of those who broke our hearts, kicked us further down when we were already low. And those who laughed in our faces at our dreams and aspirations. Because haven't they made us so much stronger in some kind of way? Appreciate the little things that people do for you. It's usually the little things that mean the most. Thank them. That is the closest you will get to kissing their hearts thank you.

A criminal called Cancer

Why do you take away lives that are not yours to take?
The innocent, the young, the old or the healthy,
the good, the lonely, the kindest souls or the wealthy.
You are a cruel vicious thing and this earth is not where
you belong.
You go around killing our loved ones,
how long will this go on?!
Your evil twisted nature,
we have all seen how you work.
A murderer in the shadows is always where you lurk.
Do you see what you do to us humans?
Do you really think this is fun?
To see someone we love become so ill?
What have you done?
Because of you there are
childless mothers and often a motherless child
all victims of your horrific crimes
and all the while,
you carry on endlessly ruining lives.
My friend, day by day, is losing her hair, it contrasts
massively to the endless curls that used to be there.
My uncle, he is sick,
has no energy and is always in pain
I don't think he'll ever smile the same way again.

You invade and intrude our bodies like it is your territory
and we think our strong defence is a treatment called
chemotherapy.

We do cake sales, sponsored walks and runs to stand up to
you because of all the distress that you put us through.
We raise money for the research
because one day you will be defeated.
I can't believe that you thought that you could even try
and beat us.
We're going to tear you down and kill you off, just like
you did to some of us.
All you've ever done is turn people's lives into a hell.
You're a criminal, Cancer, who needs to be locked forever
in your cell.

Cure your sorrows

I imagine that you watch the raindrops
roll delicately down the window pane.
I imagine that you read books
to fill the silence of your day.
I imagine that you search
for the pots of gold at the end of rainbows.
I imagine that you listen
to music just to cure your sorrows.

Your daily dose of love

Appreciate those around you,
give them hugs on a daily,
show you care about them on a daily,
support them on a daily because life's
too short,
to not let your love spread daily and
we all need our daily dose of love.

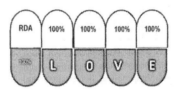

Expectations

Too many people are afraid of not being good enough
for the job that they want,
for the lover that they love,
for the mother that gave them life and brought them
into this world.
But that mindset doesn't get you very far
and it doesn't allow you to raise the bar
of what you expect from yourself
or what you want to achieve.
You can make something of yourself and impress
so many people in the process,
but if you're not happy, what difference will it make?
What would be the sake of it all in the first place?
Do not be afraid of the wonderful being that you are;
the wonderful being that has so much to offer and
who can succeed in anything that you put your mind to or
excel in the things that you've always aspired to.
Because when you do what you love, all the rest will follow.
The job that you wanted, they will take you on,
the lover that you loved, they will reciprocate the emotion,
and the mother that gave you life
and brought you into this world; she will be proud.
And yourself?
You will be happy.

Eternal love

I know that I could never forget the butterflies that you made me feel. But I'm sure, that they'll spread their wings and find another place to land. Still to this day, I will always think of you as my, 'First Love' and not my 'First Heartbreak' because there is still so much love that we share together. Like our interests, and dislikes and the genuine care that we have for one another. And there are so many things in life that remind me of you.

Everyday.

That even if we've drifted.

Our love will surely stay.

Writers

I don't want to write like other writers.
I only want to be inspired by them.

Always love, sweetly

You speak words of lavender;
sweet on the tip of your tongue.
They sound soft to my ears.
And I am always hungry for love
because I need to be full enough to reciprocate it.
Please teach me how
to always love, sweetly.

Complexity

I remember when you said
you were a bad boy; a rebel.
A boy who wanted to pave his own destiny.
I remember when you talked of all these aspirations
while still being stuck in a box called,
'Society's expectations.'
And I thought,
that's a complexity,
great enough to kill you.

Sweet temptations

I don't hate you.
I just hate myself when I'm with you.
And all the sweet temptations
you tempt me with.
I'd rather follow rules and an instruction book
but in your presence
I only crave self-destruction – look
I just want a little taste of danger
without being caught up in a fire.
I just want to live life on the edge
and know you'll catch me
if I fall to my knees.
Let me dress like a rainbow
but promise me
you'll help me hide from the bees.

What is it you hate about yourself?

You're so silly,
but sweet and
intelligent and
caring and crazy
and kind and
handsome and
spontaneous and
adventurous and strong.
Tell me what it is that you hate about yourself again?

New beginnings

Here's to new beginnings. A fresh start.
To moments of joy and happiness that last a lifetime.
To moments of sadness that only last a minute long because
they don't make your soul smile. Here's to new beginnings
where laughter plays on your lips and your eyes crease with
cheer and content. Here's to new beginnings where friends
are true and their intentions for you, are pure; beyond
words' expression. Here's to new beginnings where your
one true love reciprocates the feelings you feel for them;
and brings you bouquets of flowers as a gift of their love.
Here's to new beginnings that you have only imagined.
I hope they all come true.

Afterword

Autumn 2018.
A collection of artistic writings including poetry
and prose, all for you.

I am so happy that I have been able to publish my own poetry book. This is such a great way to express my passion for writing and I am so glad that it was made possible. I have so many people to thank for encouraging me to get where I am today and helping to make all this a success. Many thanks go to all my friends to whom I showed my poems to and to those who inspired and encouraged me to keep writing more. Some friends include Megan Nelson, Ewa Skotak, Logan Durand, Leoni Powell, Fiazah Ali, Kiko Giles, Ramsha Umar, and Walid Idrisnur to name a few. I am so grateful that you guys were able to patiently wait for the book to be published. It was such a long process. A special thanks to Daria Modlinska for her wonderful illustrations that helped make the poems come to life. Thank you to my Auntie Rita for designing the book cover and to my Uncle Philip (aka Multiple Gherkins haha!) for your endless support. Thank you to the Dyslexia Association Trust, for your support and for believing in me. I will always be very grateful. Lastly, and most importantly, I want to thank my mom (aka, my personal editor) because without you, none of this would have been possible. Thank you for putting up with my constant nagging and asking, "When do you think the book will be finished?" non-stop and for initiating the creation of this book.

Eight questions

1. How did you begin writing and did you always want to become a writer?

I come from a naturally artistic family and I began writing when I was as young as four years old. I used to write so many stories on paper that my mom would say "There is enough paper here, it's a fire hazard!" hence why I got my first laptop. I also used to take notebooks from around the house, so I could write my stories or do song writing so I could sing with my guitar. At the age of eleven, I won a poetry competition which made me so happy because I hadn't expected to win. The prize was a trip to a rugby game which I went to with my dad. At thirteen, I took part in a writing club at school called, 'First Story' and was featured alongside my friends, in the published anthology book called, 'The Chocolate Box.' I remember watching 'Sister Act' as a child and what sister Mary Clarence said to Rita Watson always stayed in my head, "if you wake up in the morning, and can't think anything but singing, you should be a singer, girl." I felt the same way about writing. I guess deep down, yes, I always wanted to be an author (and an English teacher and dancer part time haha!) But as I got older I realised that writing stories was my way of escaping a hard time I was going through, so I held onto that.

2. What were the books you most liked in your childhood?

Growing up I wanted to read the thick Harry Potter books, but I remember how my older sister said it would be too difficult for me and that I wouldn't understand it. And still to this day, I have never read them. However, my favourite books from my childhood include, 'The Famous Five Adventures Collection' by Enid Blyton, 'Noughts and Crosses' by Malorie Blackman and Jaqueline Wilson books. Overall, I would say that my number one favourite book from childhood was, 'We're going on a bear hunt' by Michael Rosen.

3. Who or what gave you the courage to start writing poems?

I began writing stories before I even started writing poetry. My first memory of beginning to write poems was the competition I won at eleven years old. My poem was based on athletics and the Olympics. Last year, I hung out with a family member and when I came home I randomly wanted to write about the day in poetry form. From here, I kept going with it and wrote many more. I think that it is quite ironic how at this time I had joined athletics again. I think some of the most significant things that gave me the courage to write poems were Instagram quotes/poetry accounts and artsy accounts too.

4. What do you find difficult about the artistic process of writing a poem?

I know it is something so simple, but I struggle with giving my poems a title. I find it hard because I want the actual poem to reveal more than the title does. It's hard to make the poem titles catchy and creative. However, I definitely want to work on making the titles more intriguing for the reader.

5. Who are your top three favourite modern poets?

I have many favourite writers, but my top three favourite modern poets are Reyna Biddy, Rupi Kaur and Nayyirah Waheed. I really like the way that they can write with such deep emotion on matters that we go through in our daily lives. They can write about such simple things yet make it a beautiful piece of art through poetry or prose.

6. Are your poems based on your real-life experiences?

Some of my poems are based on real-life experiences; some are inspired by the experiences of people close to me, aesthetical images that I've seen, music and my own thoughts and emotions.

7. What does literary success look like to you?

For me, I think being successful in my writing would mean being able to make my reader feel emotion or like they can connect on an emotional level, with what I have written. It would also mean to be able to keep improving on whatever I write. There are always opportunities for me to be better. I'd love to be able to make people feel like I have helped them through my writing because it is writing that helped me through my hard time too.

8. What are your words of encouragement for other writers that are your age or younger?

My advice would be not to be afraid of being yourself. Write because you enjoy it not because you're obligated to do it or want to follow a trend. Be inspired by everything and know that there is always room to improve on what you write. Learn to write about different topics or emotions that you don't feel confident about, so you can develop. Most importantly, understand that there are always going to be people that don't like what or how you write but don't be discouraged by this as there will always be people that do – and if you write for your own benefit then you won't need to be disheartened by another people's dislike. As Nayyirah Waheed says, "Be an artist made of art, not made of other people's worship or scorn, that's too volatile, too wearing, too empty, too full."

37328193R00144

Printed in Great Britain
by Amazon